100 POEMS SO SHORT
YOU JUST CAN'T FORGET
THEM!

Paul Cookson: A Short Biography

Paul was born and is still alive.
He edits and writes lots of poems.
He performs all over the place.
His favourite shorts are football shorts (white).
He is never short of material for his poems
And will be doing loads more books . . .
Shortly.

Jane Eccles: A Short Biography

Jane is an illustrator.
She lives in London.
She has a husband and a son.
And a cat called Wilfred.

Dedicated to all the staff and pupils
at Woodlands Junior School, Doncaster

First published 2000 by Macmillan Children's Books

This edition published 2001 by Macmillan Children's Books
a division of Macmillan Publishers Limited
20 New Wharf Road, London N1 9RR
Basingstoke and Oxford
www.panmacmillan.com

Associated companies throughout the world

ISBN 0 330 48266 1

3 5 7 9 8 6 4 2

A CIP catalogue record for this book is available from the British Library

Printed and bound in Great Britain by Mackays of Chatham plc, Kent

Contents

Fishing

There is a fine
line

between fishing
and standing
on the bank
like an idiot.

Gerard Benson

Names

Bill, Ben, Cliff or Ken,
Mary, Moira and Mick.
Bob, Beth, Jess or Jen,
Nellie, Norah and Nick.

Ali, Alex, Leon or Les,
Sunil, Selwyn and Sam.
Abdul, Ago, Daphne or Des,
Pauline, Patti and Pam.

Things just wouldn't be the same
Had we a number instead of a name.

Redvers Brandling

Just a Small War

We're watching the usual war pictures
On the six o'clock news on the box:
Shells exploding, bodies lying,
Fires, tanks, roadblocks.
Dave says, ''Course, that's just a small war.
I'm not sure who's fighting who.
For *real* wars you have to go back
To World Wars One and Two.'

On the screen, in her shattered house,
A woman picks around for her stuff.

Bet she doesn't think it's a small war.
Bet she thinks it's real enough.

Eric Finney

Flowers

Flowers are soft, they smell of aunties,
weeds are better – no one shouts
if you pull off all their petals
or stamp them flat into the ground.

Grown-ups are funny about their garden,
they don't see it like I do –
'Such lovely flowers', they say, when really
it's a jungle where toy soldiers hide.

Leaves are alright, you can kick them
and make smoke signals when they burn;
but what I like best in a garden
is trees to climb, fat slugs, and worms.

Dave Calder

A Recipe for a Magical Day at the Seaside

Take one beach, soak in sunshine,
gently drop jewels into rock pools,
add the promise
of buried treasure.

Season with sandcastles
and the sound of a seagull's song,
mix in melting ice cream, sinking sand,
stories of mermaids and one old shipwreck.

Finally, add children.
Then watch and wait.

Andrew Collett

The Spotted Grumble Bug

Living up every teacher's nose
curled up nice and snug,
lives a most amazing creature:
The Spotted Grumble Bug.

It's there to make your teacher cross,
it's there to make him cruel,
for all teachers have the bug
whenever they're at school.

So, if you see your teacher twitch,
if his anger really shows,
remember, it's just the Grumble Bug,
picking at his nose.

Andrew Collett

Early in the Morning

Early in the morning
The water hits the rocks,
The birds are making noises
Like alarm clocks,
The soldier on the skyline
Fires a golden gun
And over the back of the chimney-stack
Explodes the silent sun.

Charles Causley

Dark Day

Lamp-posts stand like sparklers
spitting rays of light into the night,

blobs of yellow jellyfish
wriggle in pathway puddles.

Bullets of rain ricochet,
run rivers in sleeve creases,

make lakes across boxed lunches
of crushed crisps, sandwiches,

clutched by huddled children
on a dark day way to school.

Gina Douthwaite

Who'll Go, If You'll Go

Do you know Hugo?
He'll go if I'll go
And Hugh'll go, if you'll go.
So . . . Hugo'll go and Hugh'll go
If I go and you go
That's who'll go, if you'll go.

John Foster

Hippoportant Poem ...

A hippopotamus

Would squash a lot of us

If it sat on us.

Mike Harding

Digging For It

Sometimes a poem is less of an invention
and more of a find
its birth a kind
of archaeology,
a job of unearthing and piecing together
and sometimes a piece won't fit
because it's part of something else,
and sometimes it's just a bit of old rubbish.

John Hegley

Our Tree

It takes so long for a tree to grow
So many years of pushing the sky.

Long branches stretch the arms
Reach out with their wooden fingers.

Years drift by, fall like leaves
From green to yellow then back to green.

Since my grandad was a boy
And then before his father's father

There's been an elm outside our school
Its shadow long across our playground.

Today three men ripped it down.
Chopped it up. It took ten minutes.

David Harmer

Recipes

To make a cake
Take
½ lb flour

To make a summer pudding
Put
In a basin
Some bread and soak

To make a summer
Take
Half an hour
Soak
In the sun that is squeezing through a gap in the
  houses

Shut your eyes
And your summer is ready.

Jenny Joseph

Help!

Our dentist's old chair
was a sit-you-up
now-let-me-look
sort of chair.

But his new one has
a button to push
and all of a sudden
you're flat
on your back
and he's
leaning over
like Drac.

Patricia Leighton

Dick's Dog

Dick had a dog
The dog dug
The dog dug deep
How deep did Dick's dog dig?

Dick had a duck
The duck dived
The duck dived deep
How deep did Dick's duck dive?

Dick's duck dived as deep as Dick's dog dug.

Trevor Millum

Emergencies

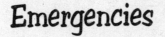

Red Alert! Red Alert!
I've dropped my lolly in the dirt.

S.O.S! S.O.S!
I've spilled some custard
down my dress.

999! 999!
My bike's got tangled
in the washing line.

Ring the alarm! Ring the alarm!
There's an insect landing on my arm.

Bring First Aid! Bring First Aid!
There's a beetle in my lemonade.

Ambulance! And make it quick!
I think I'm going to be sick.

Tony Mitton

Coming Out of the Cinema in the Afternoon

I think
I'm still
in the film
and I'm blinking;

I blink,
I'm a still
from the film
and I'm thinking

'Keep still
don't blink
keep thinking
and the film

will still
keep blinking
as I'm thinking
I'm the film.'

Ian McMillan

Mum Says . . .

Eat up your apple,
eat your ice cream,
eat up your jelly,
your strawberry-dream!
Eat up your biscuits
and chocolate cake,
your trifle and cream
for goodness' sake
or you'll get

NO

CABBAGE!

Judith Nicholls

Basil

When Cousin Basil
Played his bassoon
His body blew up
Like a barrage balloon
When I asked him shouldn't
He suck not blow
He swiftly answered
NOOOOOOOOOOOOOOOOOOOOOOOOOOOOOOOOOOOOOO
OOOOOOOOOOOOOOOOOOOOOOOOOOOOOOOOOOOOO
OOOOOOOOOOOOOOOOOOOOOOOOOOOOOOOOOOOOO
OOOOOOOOOOOOOOOOOOOOOOOOOOOOOOOOOOOOO
OOOOOOOOOOOOOOOOOOOOOOOO
OOOOOOOOOOOOOOOO
OOOOOOOO
OOOO
OO
O
  O
   O
    O
     O
      O
       O
        O
         O
          O

Gareth Owen

19

Short Poem

I am a very tiny verse,

Noticed by no one at all,

My ending is unhappy

Because I am so sma

Andrew Fusek Peters

After the Storm

Shells shattered
by the storm tide

Blown deckchairs
on the brown waves

Flung pebbles
on the pavement

Gull dabbles
in the paddling pool

Rain drizzles
on the car park

Lights dazzle
in the arcade

Rita Ray

I'm Carrying
the Baby

Paul was three.
'Look at me,' he said,
'look at me
I'm carrying the baby.
Look at me
look at me
I'm carrying the baby.'

'Oh,' said Paul,
'look at me
I've dropped the baby.'

Michael Rosen

Batgirl's Day Off

Auntie Betty pulls her cloak on
And the mask – the one with ears
Then she goes and does the shopping
In her bashed-up Cavalier
All the people down at Tescos
Bow and curtsey in the aisles
And the queue for autographs
Goes round the block for miles and miles.

But Betty waves them all away
'Sorry. It's my day off today.'

Andrea Shavick

Wait

These are
the good
old days.

Just wait
and see.

Steve Turner

Norman Norton's Nostrils

Oh, Norman Norton's nostrils
Are powerful and strong;
Hold on to your belongings
If he should come along.

And do not ever let him
Inhale with all his might,
Or else your pens and pencils
Will disappear from sight.

Right up his nose they'll vanish;
Your future will be black.
Unless he gets the sneezes,
You'll never get them back!

Colin West

On the Pavement

Sauntering along alone I hear other busier footsteps
   behind me.
Not feeling threatened but awkward
I wonder, should I slow down my walking
and let them get by as soon as possible
or shall I imperceptibly quicken to a higher gear
before they are near enough to notice?
Ah, it's OK, it sounds like they've just fallen over.

John Hegley

Who's Who

I used to think nurses
Were women,
I used to think police
Were men,
I used to think poets
Were boring,
Until I became one of them.

Benjamin Zephaniah

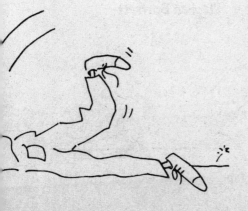

Just Doing

Your legs know how to walk

Your eyes know how to cry

Your mouth knows how to talk

Your heart knows how to fly.

Stephen Bowkett

In the Kitchen

In the kitchen
After the aimless
Chatter of the plates,
The murmurings of the gas,
The chuckle of the water pipes
And the sharp exchanges
Of knives, forks and spoons,
Comes the serious quiet,
When the sink slowly clears its throat
And you can hear the occasional rumble
Of the refrigerator's tummy
As it digests the cold.

John Cotton

Imagination

There's a horrible thing in the wardrobe,
That comes out when I turn off the light,
There's a thing by my bed
With fingers just waiting,
To tickle my toes in the night.
There's a thing in the garden that
Howls at the moon,
A thing in the hall dark and grim,
'It's just your Imagination, that's all,' says Mum –

I don't like the sound of him.

David Orme

Lim

There once was a bard of Hong Kong
Who thought limericks were too long.

Gerard Benson

Batman's Exercise Video

Pull on the tights
Yeah, pull on the tights
Pull up the trunks
Yeah, pull up the trunks

I said   twirl the cape
          twirl the cape
          twirl the cape
          twirl the cape

Pull on the boots
Yeah, pull on the boots
Snap on the mask
Yeah, snap on the mask

I said   twirl the cape
          twirl the cape
          twirl the cape
          twirl the cape

Repeat until opponents are fully dazzled . . .

Ian McMillan

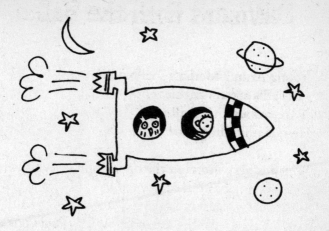

The Owl and the Astronaut

The owl and the astronaut
Sailed through space
In their intergalactic ship
They kept hunger at bay
With three pills a day
And drank through a protein drip.
The owl dreamed of mince
And slices of quince
And remarked how life had gone flat;
'It may be all right
To fly faster than light
But I preferred the boat and the cat.'

Gareth Owen

Wizard with the Ball

Young Arthur Merlin's spellbinding
His skills are crystal clear
A wizard with the ball
He makes it disappear!

Which is very useful in the opposition's penalty area.

Paul Cookson

Shocked!

Just look at you –
All studs and rings,
Those false nails
And that fake tattoo!
Your hair! My skirt!
Those boots! That hat!
No, Mum, you're NOT
Going out like that!

Sue Cowling

First Morning

I was there on that first morning of creation
when heaven and earth occupied one space
and no one had heard of the human race.

I was there on that first morning of creation
when a river rushed from the belly of an egg
and a mountain rose from a golden yolk.

I was there on the first morning of creation
when the waters parted like magic cloth
and the birds shook feathers at the first joke.

John Agard

Sporting Delusions

I'm a panther I'm an acrobat
I'm an athlete so supreme
I'm a spinning ballerina
I'm a Herculean dream

I'm a supple tightrope walker I am loose-limbed
I'm so fit
I am bendy, bouncy, leapy
every single bit

I also have my off days,
as I stand here on the line
I'm a small and tearful goalie,
and so far, I've let in nine.

Stewart Henderson

Wrong Rhymes

If all the world were paper and all the seas were ink,
I'd write a lot of fizzy pop for something nice to drink;
I'd write a lot of recipes for something good to eat,
I'd write a lot of fudgy sweets and chocolates for a treat;
I'd write a lot of answers, so I'd be a proper smartie,
I'd write a load of invitations to my birthday party;
I'd write a lot of letters to the papers and MPs,
Saying: Feed the hungry; Stop pollution; House the
    homeless, please;
I'd write a special charter saying people should be free,
I'd open all the prisons and I'd throw away the key;
I'd write a lot of hows and whens, I'd write the answer why,
I'd write a lot of poems that would make you laugh or cry.

Tony Charles

A Very Short Poem about
a Very Long Supermodel

Jerry Hall

Very tall

John Cooper Clarke

Figuratively Speaking

If I speak in pictures

Then your ears must be my canvas

And my tongue a brush that paints the words

I want you to imagine.

Paul Cookson

In Memory of Fido

Here lies Fido, Oh the Grief,

How we will miss his gnashing teeth,

Thief of all our Sunday roasts,

Pray that he's now biting ghosts!

Andrew Fusek Peters

Peach Blossoms

Peach blossoms in spring,
promising fruit in autumn.
For now I savour
confetti petals showered
like there were no tomorrow.

Debjani Chatterjee

Whatshisname

That chap who wrote lots of plays . . .
His name's on the tip of my tongue:
Wobbledart? Waggledagger?
Swaysticker? Joggleprong?
Shuddershaft? Quiverlance? Wavespike?
Not quite, but I'm getting near . . .
It's something like Jigglejavelin . . .
I've got it! His name's Shakespeare!

Eric Finney

43

The Orang-utan

The closest relative of man
They say, is the orang-utan;
And when I look at Grandpapa,
I realise how right they are.

Colin West

A Three-legged Friend

They have a three-legged dog
and they call him Clover
and sometimes he falls over
and if he'd have had four legs
maybe they'd have called him
Lucky.

John Hegley

A Little Alliteration

A little alliteration,
like 'lizards licking liquorice',
is a super sound sensation,
so snortsomeful and snickerish.
Children chewing chocolate chips
are standing at the station,
and taking turns to try to teach
a little alliteration.

Mike Jubb

Don't Talk to Strangers

Most people

are strange

because no one

ever talks to them.

Rupert Loydell

The Things Mums Say . . .

Wake up!
Get up!
Out of bed!
Mind your feet!
Mind your head!
Don't run around.
Don't be late.
Look at your room!
What a state!
Put all your stuff away now, please.
Why can I never find my keys?
Close your mouth and eat your food.

Look at that!
Don't stare it's rude.
Elbows OFF the table please
Money doesn't grow on trees.
I won't tell you again . . .
Did you hear what I said?
I won't tell you again
It's time for bed.

Michaela Morgan

Questions

. . . why does ice always feel cold
And why does anyone have to get old
And why are deserts always bone dry
And how do clouds stay up in the sky
And how do you know the earth is round
And how do worms breathe underground

And what do fishes drink
And why are snails so slow
And what do babies think
And where do shadows go

And how many drops in the ocean
And why's the horizon so far
And if atoms make up a person
Can people make up a star
And . . .

Kevin McCann

My Cousin Melda

My Cousin Melda
she don't make fun
she ain't afraid of anyone
even mosquitoes
when they bite her
she does bite them back
and say –
'Now tell me, how you like that?'

Grace Nichols

Growing Pains

Growing
    bored
Growing
    sad
Growing
    mad
Growing
    batty
Growing
    scatty
Looking
    tatty
Feeling
    ratty
Looking
    grumpy
Growing
    jumpy
Feeling
    grumpy
Growing
    spotty
Growing
    pains

Brian Patten

The Biggest and the Best

Buckdale Pike,
Garrelgum Foss,
Hag Dike
Blaydike Moss,
Cocklee Fell,
Dead Man's Cave,
Robin Hood's Well,
Giant's Grave,
Kealcup Hill,
Malham Tarn,
Bracken Gill,
New Ing Barn,
Gordale Bridge,
Settle Scar,
Winshill Ridge,
Deepdale Carr,
Knuckle Bone Pasture,
Ghaistrill's Strid,
Hawkswick Clowder,
Crutchin Gill Rigg,
In England, Ireland, Scotland, Wales,
There's nowt as grand as t' Yorkshire Dales.

Gervase Phinn

Spring Fashion Show

And now April saunters on
Loose-limbed and golden-haired
Wearing a see-through number
Of infinitely-blue, appliquéd
With fluffy white clouds.

The designer gets a standing ovation.

(Same dress every year and we still fall for it.)

Roger McGough

My Favourite Thingummybob

My favourite colour is W,
my favourite drink is bees.
My favourite song is an apple,
and my favourite hat is trees.

My favourite flower is bottle,
my favourite book is socks.
My favourite sweets are 40,
and my favourite game is a fox.

My favourite pet is a teaspoon,
my favourite friend is a clock.
My favourite clothes are biscuits,
and my favourite word is

S

P

L

O

C

K

!

John Rice

Into the Mixer

Into the mixer he went,
   the nosy boy,
into the mess of wet cement,
   round and round
   with a glugging sound
and a boyish screamed complaint.

Out of the mixer he came,
   the concrete boy,
onto the road made of the same
   quick-setting stuff.
   He looked rough
and he'd only himself to blame.

Matthew Sweeney

Stick Insect Haiku

I like stick insects

The only problem with them

Is they look like sticks

Roger Stevens

All the Stars

All the stars are tiny eyes:
They watch us as we sleep.
They watch us pull the covers up,
And dance through all our dreams.
But when we wake each morning,
The stars creep off to bed,
And like to think
As we yawn and blink,
That it's *our* eyes that shine
Like stars in the sky,
And we're watching them instead.

David Greygoose

Daffodils

Wandering along the road
By the lake, I saw a load
of golden daffodils
Ten thousand, give or take.

Now and then,
I think of them again.

Roger McGough

A certain teacher of English has accused me of plagiarizing a poem about
daffodils by William Wordsworth. I can honestly say that I have never
heard of William Wordsworth nor read his poem (which is much longer
than mine anyway).

Short Poem

Short poems
are fun.
You can see
at a glance
whether you
like them
or not.

Steve Turner

Nightmares!

'Don't eat cheese before you go to bed
Or you'll get 'em,' my grandma said.
But,
One night at supper there was cheddar for us
And I spent the night with a brontosaurus.

Redvers Brandling

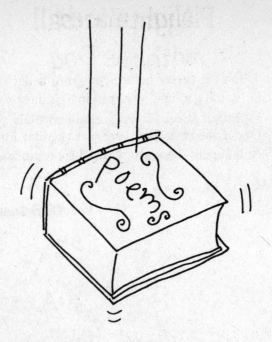

Heavy Reading

This book of poems
is very weighty;
full of sad verses
that will bring
tears to your eyes.
Even more so
if you drop it
on your foot.

John C. Desmond

Playing Football
with the Dog

Arthur Sneer played football with his dog.

How cruel can you get?

Brian Patten

Doctor Frankenstein's Complete Make-over Service

Eyebrows plucked tummy tucked
Eyelids lifted, blemishes shifted
Buttocks hitched, lost hair re-stitched
Neck tightened, cheekbones heightened, pupils brightened
Legs extended, nose unbended, ears amended.

You'll look a picture of perfect health
But you won't look like your old self.

John Coldwell

Questions

Who likes to swing from
The branch of a tree?

I DO!

Who likes cheeseburgers
With baked beans for tea?

I DO!

Who likes to watch
What comes on the TV?

I DO!

Who likes to tidy up my bedroom,
Fetch the shopping, cook the lunch
And do the washing up?

MUM DOES!

Doesn't she . . .?

Trevor Harvey

Halloween's Coming

Halloween's coming,
The pumpkin's getting fat.
Please put a spider
in the goblin's hat.

If you haven't got a spider
A beetle will do.
If you haven't got a beetle . . .
Then look out for the ghoul!

Dave Ward and Emily

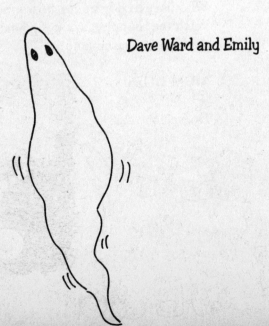

Glow-worm

I know a worried glow-worm,
I wonder what the matter is?
He seems so glum and gloomy,
Perhaps he needs new batteries!

Colin West

Sinister Symphony

Warlocks whisper
Coffins creak
Tombstones tumble
Spirits speak

Phantoms frolic
Monsters moan
Serpents slither
Gremlins groan

Crones cackle
Demons dance
Am I staying?
Not a chance!

Paul Bright

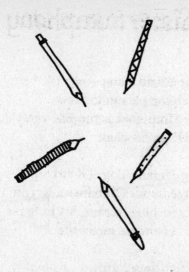

This Little Poem

This little poem has five lines
and five words on every line.
I wrote it out five times
between five o'clock and five past nine
using five different pencils every time
and this little poem tells lies.

Ian McMillan

Superman's Dog

Superman's dog – he's the best
Helping pets in distress
Red and gold pants and vest
'SD' on his chest

Superman's dog – X-ray sight
Green bones filled with Kryptonite
Bright blue lycra tights in flight
Faster than a meteorite

Better than Batman's Robin
Rougher than Robin's bat
Faster than Spiderman's spider
Cooler than Catwoman's cat

Superman's dog – bionic scent
Crime prevention – his intent
Woof and tough – cement he'll dent
What's his name – Bark Kent!

Paul Cookson

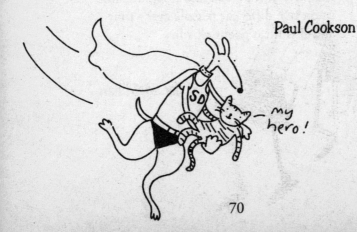

– my
hero!

Shame

There's a girl at school
we teased today;
made jokes, called her names.
My friends all laughed,
called it harmless fun,
said it was just a game.

Now I'm at home
feeling horrid inside,
long gone that thoughtless grin.
How will I face her
tomorrow at school?
I wish I hadn't joined in.

Tracey Blance

Overheard in a Doctor's Waiting Room

'Ha! Taking a week off?'
'Heart aching; a wee cough.'

Gerard Benson

Mum Used Prittstick

Mum used Prittstick
Instead of lipstick
Then went and kissed my dad.

Two days passed
Both stuck fast.
The longest snog they ever had.

Paul Cookson

Interesting

I have lots of interests –
my lego, my train set,
my bike, my football.
My hobby is watching my dad
play with them all.

Dave Calder

Premonition

before	I saw it	I knew	I'd seen it	before
I saw it	I knew	I'd seen it	before	I saw it
I knew	I'd seen it	before	I saw it	I knew
I'd seen it	before	I saw it	I knew	I'd seen it
before	I saw it	I knew	I'd seen it	before

John Carley

The Sorrow of Socks

Some socks are loners –
They can't live in pairs.
On washdays they've shown us
They want to be loners.
They puzzle their owners,
They hide in dark lairs.
Some socks are loners –
They won't live in pairs.

Wendy Cope

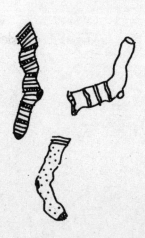

All Day Saturday

Let it sleet on Sunday,
Monday let it snow,
Let the mist on Tuesday
From the salt-sea flow.
Let it hail on Wednesday,
Thursday let it rain,
Let the wind on Friday
Blow a hurricane,
But Saturday, Saturday
Break fair and fine
And all day Saturday
Let the sun shine.

Charles Causley

School Trip

I saw a man in a cardboard box
I saw a lady too,
Her head was wrapped in paper,
She only had one shoe.
We went and saw where Nelson is
We visited St Paul's,
We visited the Palace
and we climbed the city walls.

We saw the Tower Bridge open,
We went and saw Big Ben

. . . but I remember ladies
and boxes full of men.

Peter Dixon

Pets' Palindrome

Cats hate dogs.
Arch backs, threatening;
Scratch,
Claws unsheathed,
Dangerous
Unsheathed claws
Scratch,
Threatening backs arch.
Dogs hate cats!

Pam Gidney

Emily's Love Poem

Jason is so romantic
yesterday in class
he punched me on the arm
He's so romantic
he punched me again at lunch

I think he likes me.

Jason's Love Poem

Emily kept looking at me in class
so I punched her,
not hard, on the arm.
She looked at me at lunch
so I punched her again

I think she likes me.

Steven Herrick

A Poem for my Cat

You're black and sleek and beautiful

What a pity your best friends won't tell you

Your breath smells of Kit-E-Kat.

Adrian Henri

Ultrasonnet
(To be made into a Möbius strip.*)

Bats!
chitter
chatter
twitter
critter
skitter
flutter
flitter
jitter
zigger
zagger
quicker
gnatter
fitter
fatter
Bats!

Mike Johnson

* A Möbius strip is a strip of paper given a half-twist and then glued end-to-end. This forms a belt-shaped loop – with only one surface.

Ancient Aunts

Auntie Alice's
Auntie Amy's
Auntie Annie
IS
Aunt Eek

Craig King

The Spoon Music Man

My uncle
made music with spoons.

He could play
any number of tunes.

He banged them
on knees and his nose.

He banged them
on elbows and toes.

My uncle
made wonderful tunes.

He made
magical music with spoons.

Wes Magee

Our House

It's 10 minutes walk from the 8 o'clock train
It's got 9 windows with 23 panes

It's got 8 rooms with 15 chairs
There's 7 people with a million hairs

It's got 6 beds with 13 heads
There's 5 animals with 18 legs

It's got 4 bookshelves with 50 books
And 3 mirrors with a thousand looks

It's got 2 gates with broken locks
And 1 front door with a brass letter box!

Trevor Millum

An Interesting
Fact About One
of my Relatives

My

great great great great
great great great great
great great great great
great great great great
great great great great
great great great great
great great great great

grandad is very old.

Ian McMillan

Incident in New York City

The Department of Superheroes
heard a desperate telephone plea.
'Bring needle and thread,' a stern voice said.
'And bring them here to me.'

Then the voice explained what had happened
and how circumstances were dire:
Superman had just torn his tights
on the Empire State Building's spire.

Brian Moses

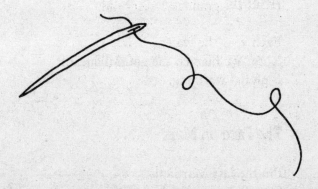

A Bit of a Mystery

Pyramids

Even paperweights
This big won't stop the desert
Blowing everywhere.

Stonehenge

Thunder in the hills:
Watch out! here comes the ogre –
He's lost his false teeth.

Atlantis

Each year the water
Rose. We blamed the gods. You call
It global warming.

The Face on Mars

I'm the last Martian:
Some joker covered me up
Sleeping on the beach.

David Orme

Revenge

My brother chased me with a crab,

He found it by a rock,

But I *will* get my own back –

It's now inside his sock!

Coral Rumble

The Worst Tree-Climber in the World

My brother is the worst tree-climber in the world!
Well let's just say,
he's the slowest tree-climber in the world.
And today he wants to climb the horse chestnut tree
at the bottom of our garden.
You see he is after the conkers.

Now Mum said he shouldn't
because it's too high
and there aren't any conkers yet!
But I say he should
because it's high
and there might be by the time he gets there!

Ian Souter

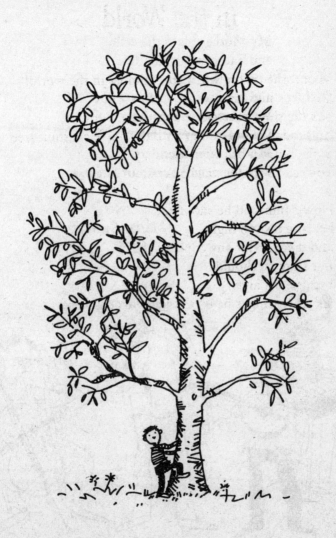

A Musical Family

My Mother plays the cello
and Father toots the flute.
I prefer the organ
and my brother strums a lute.
We practise all together.
We practise every day.
Mother often wonders
why the neighbours moved away.

Marian Swinger

Neversaurus

When dinosaurs roamed the earth,

So huge it was easy to spot 'em.

You'd frequently see a triceratops,

But never a tricerabottom.

Celia Warren

In Two Minds

Half of me wants
to say 'Yes.'
Half of me wants
to say 'No.'
So, although
it's nice of you
to ask,
I feel I
can only say
'Yo.'*

*I might decide to alter that to 'Nes.'

Bernard Young

Up in Smoke

Cornelius loved Chemistry
It had a strange attraction
The final words he spoke were 'Sir,
Is this a chain reaction?'

Paul Bright

Puzzle

I thought I was the biggest child

in our little family,

but Mum says Dad's the biggest child

so where does that leave me?

Brian Moses

Flower Power

We planted some bulbs in our garden

in straight lines, row by row

and, although they're not very pretty

they do give off a wonderful glow.

Andrew Collett

Fifteen Words about my Nephew

Pink!

Popped
Out
Early

Gummy
Grin

Eyes
Marbles

Fingers
Fragile

Champion
Dribbler

First
Word

DADADADADADADADUGH!!

Simon Pitt

Grow a Poem

Find some words
to make a poem
Shake them up and
watch them growing

Drop some more in
move them round
How do they look?
How do they sound?

What's its rhythm?
Should it rhyme?
Is it ready?
Is it fine?

Read it
Say it
Sing it now
Try it softly
Try it LOUD!

James Carter

Rhymes

The trouble with rhymes
That you find sometimes
Is that once
They are found
You find you are bound
Just because of the sound
To use them and then
You never know when
To stop!

Pie Corbett

Run, Run!

Run, Run –
Here comes Mum,
She's got porridge in her hair.

Run, Run –
Here comes Mum,
She's found the spider on her chair.

Run, Run –
Here comes Mum,
And she knows who put it there!

Dave Ward

My Sari

Saris hang on the washing line:
a rainbow in our neighbourhood.
This little orange one is mine,
it has a mango leaf design.
I wear it as a Rani would.
It wraps around me like sunshine,
it ripples silky down my spine,
and I stand tall and feel so good.

Debjani Chatterjee

Poem For Sale

Poem For Sale
(One careful owner)
With simile
(as lucky as a dime)
Two exquisite
And erudite adjectives
And one rhyme
Going
For a song

Roger Stevens

Acknowledgements

The compiler and publishers wish to thank the individual poets and the following for permission to use the poems in this book:

Gerard Benson: 'Lim', first published in *Does It Trouble You?*, Puffin 1995; 'Fishing', first published in *Evidence of Elephants*, Viking, 1995; 'Overheard in a Doctor's Waiting Room', first published in the *New Statesman*; Charles Causley: 'All Day Saturday' and 'Early in the Morning', by permission of David Higham Associates; John Cotton: 'In the Kitchen', first published in *The Crystal Zoo*, Oxford University Press, 1985; Gina Douthwaite: 'Dark Day', first published in *From Us to You*, Hodder, 1997; John Hegley: 'Digging for It', 'On the Pavement' and 'Three-legged Friend' reprinted by permission of PFD; Stewart Henderson: 'Sporting Delusions', first published in *Who Left Grandpa at the Chip Shop?*, Lion Books, 2000; Jenny Joseph: 'Recipes' from *All the Things I See*, Macmillan Children's Books, 2000; Brian Moses: Puzzle, previously published in *Rice, Pie and Moses / An Odd Kettle of Fish*, Macmillan Children's Books; Coral Rumble: 'Revenge' first published in *Creatures, Teachers and Family Features* by Coral Rumble, Macdonald Young Books, 1999; Steve Turner: 'Short Poem' and 'Wait', first published in *Up to Date* by Steve Turner, Hodder & Stoughton, 1983, 1993; Dave Ward: 'Run, Run!', previously published in *Twinkle Twinkle Chocolate Bar*, OUP, 1991; Celia Warren: 'Neversaurus', first published in *Penny Whistle Pete*, Collins Educational, 1995; Bernard Young: 'In Two Minds', first published in *Double Talk*, Stonecreek Press, 1994.